A Children's Book About

BEING CARELESS

Managing Editor: Ellen Klarberg
Copy Editor: Annette Gooch
Editorial Assistant: Lana Eberhard
Art Director: Jennifer Wiezel
Production Artist: Gail Miller
Illustration Designer: Bartholomew
Inking Artist: Susie Hornig
Coloring Artist: Susie Hornig
Lettering Artist: Linda Hanney
Typographer: Communication Graphics

A Children's Book About

BEING CARELESS

By Joy Berry

GROLIER ENTERPRISES CORP.

This book is about Lennie.

Reading about Lennie can help you understand and deal with **being careless**.

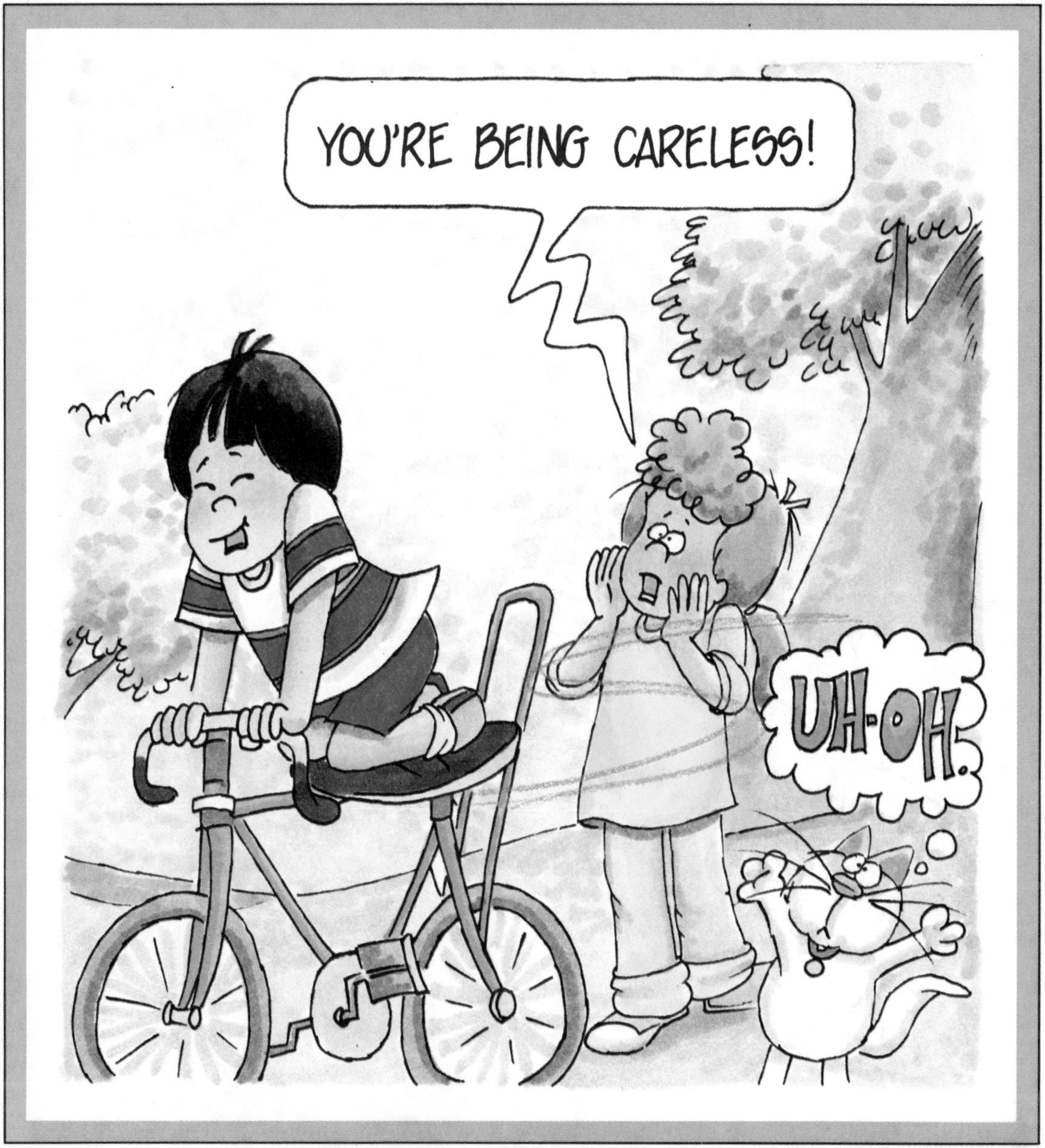
YOU'RE BEING CARELESS!
UH-OH.

You are being careless when you act as if you do not care about yourself.

You are being careless when you act as if you do not care about the people and things around you.

Being careless can cause you to hurt yourself.

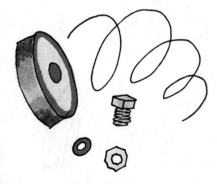

Being careless can cause you to hurt other people.

Being careless can cause you to damage or destroy things.

It is not good to be careless.

You need to *be careful* instead.

When you are careful, you act as if you care about yourself.

When you are careful, you act as if you care about the people and things around you.

Be careful.

Obey the rules.

Your parents usually know what you need to do to keep yourself and others safe. They usually know what you need to do to take care of the things around you.

The rules they make can help you be careful.

Be careful.

Pay attention to what you do so you will make fewer mistakes.

Be careful.

Slow down so you can avoid accidents and mistakes that happen when you hurry.

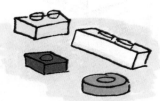

Be careful.

Watch where you are going so you can avoid tripping and bumping into things.

Be careful.

Be aware of people and things around you so you can avoid dangerous situations.

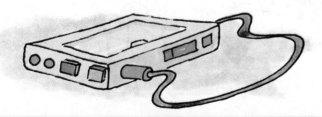

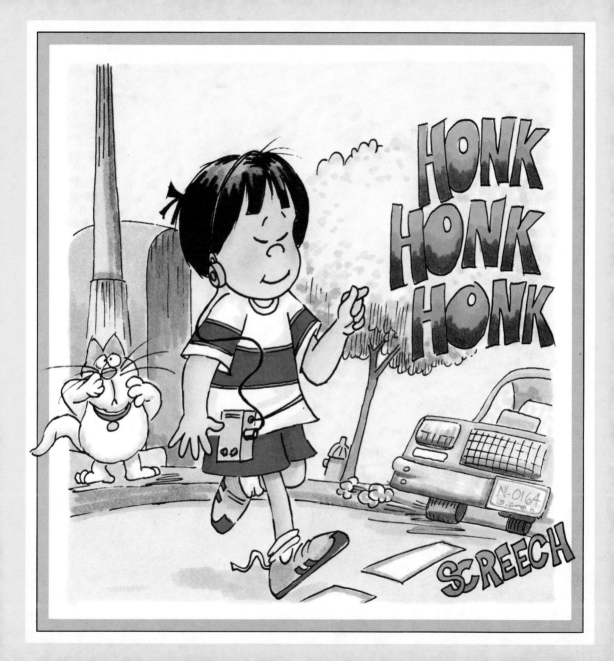

Be careful.

Avoid playing roughly so no one will get hurt and nothing will get broken.

Be careful.

Avoid playing with dangerous things so you
will not hurt yourself or others.

Be careful.

Avoid playing in dangerous places so you will not hurt yourself or others.

Being careless is not good for you or the people around you.

It is better when you are careful.